the things I felt but didn't say in therapy

Lauren Delgado

published by CK Publishing Co.,Ltd

The only thing the author holds onto as the core of this book is giving.

Thank you for giving yourself a chance to pick up this book in your hands.

Thank you for giving this book a chance to be seen, no matter by posting it on your Instagram, Tiktok, Facebook, and other social media.

Thank you for letting the author express her feelings through these raw and real words.

Contents;

It's been three years since I started telling
words and thoughts you won't hear as I can't even speak a thing
to anyone, so I've been keeping this pain with me
quietly, but now I know what it means to be brave, so I share my feelings only to those who don't understand to try
to get what I'm dealing with all this time and for those who are suffering to smile and to know, you're not alone in this crime
and we'll get through it together when the sun shines.

About depression

;

(:

:(

Trigger warning: death, suicide & depression

It's me whom to blame for why the depression made me feel ashamed
as I can't take it down.

Am I that unlucky?
Why do I have to suffer?
I just want to be happy
but my brain can't weather.

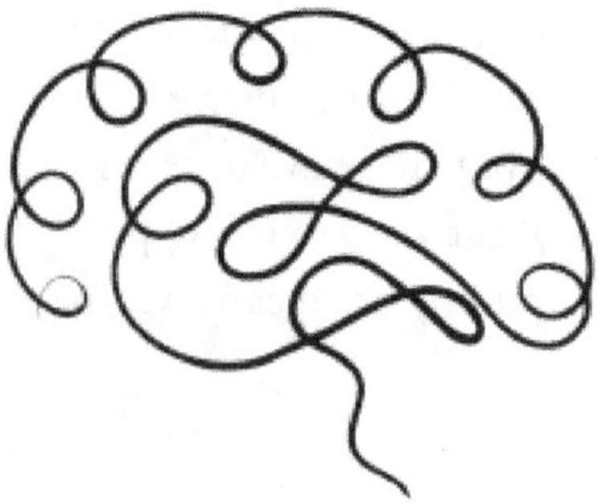

Only a depressed person knows it better

than others who try to understand depression and many seem to get it and accept those who encounter but they actually don't fully grasp the aggravation.

In front is the psychiatrist who's been by my side she always nods and listens to my stories humbly but even she doesn't feel what I'm trying to survive

"Be patient, take medicine, and keep going", says she normally.

...

Then I leave the therapy room, sighing weakly.

Every morning you get up and shower

stand in front and give a big smile at the mirror to the person in front of you and say,

'I love you!"

and remember that they love you the most with no clues.

Don't forget to love yourself even how hard it is for your day because only you will always stay by your side till old and grey.

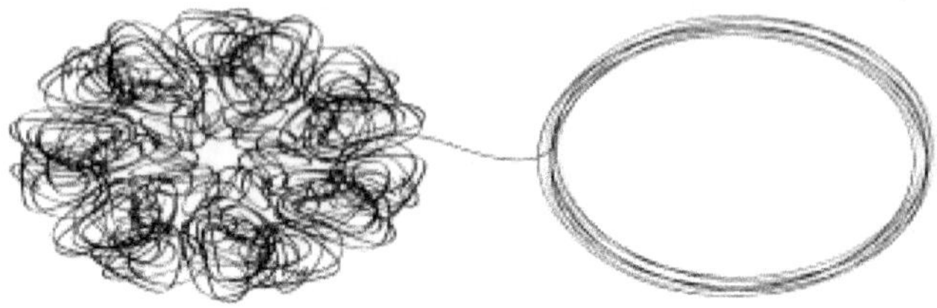

Time flies slowly with this in me most of it is such a horrible nightmare
but not all is terrifying and scary.
I can still spend some good times with care.

Depression sucks!
Only we know and feel it
I just want to be loved and freed
keep aware of my thoughts and admit
we can beat this beast even my strength is wee.

I guess you also want to run away to a faraway, sacred city and pray
where depression can't find your soul and wish you hadn't met it, this ghoul that eats you alive and watches you die even ghosts can't scare you out of mind.

But in the end, you know you can't really run.

You have to bear with it for your whole life

no matter how much it swallows you with its fun. I barely remember when was the last time

I was truly happy through my poor little memory. It's been so long time since I last smiled.

The darkness is killing me inside, painfully and I know you also feel my suffering cries.

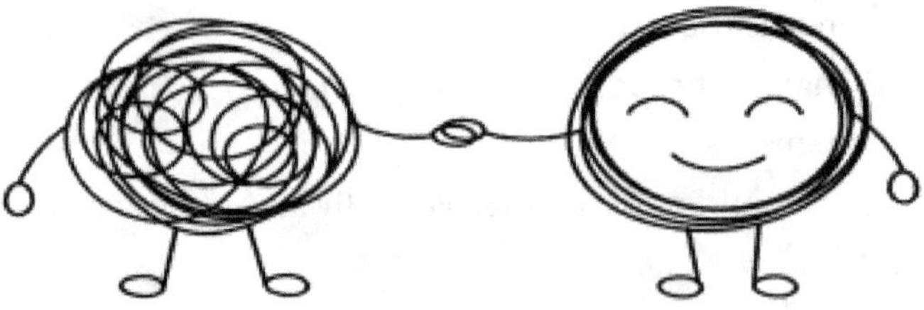

You can deceive yourself for a short time that you are just sick as depression farms inside your little mind, by admitting it wholeheartedly.

You can be cured by time and care from your company.

Yet, I don't want to think or fake myself that

.

I'm normal

.

because my inside is screaming, I'm not OKAY at all!

They ask me, "Are you okay?" "I'm fine because of the pills," I say
They tell me I look better But the truth is I never
ever feel okay with this in mind.
Just want people I love to confide I don't want to express
my pain from losing the chest of ability to feel happy.
I'm like the weak who even can't enjoy the little things like I ever can.

It'll be soon morning
I cling to my wish all night even now I can't feel anything
but darkness that kills me inside.

Depression always drives you to death

as you don't want to hold any more breath and you don't want to feel any more pain that chains you to the touch of flames burning inside your little mind.

You always think of the way to die but believe me, you can take over it like playing in a racing game of sh*t.

Sometimes you lose, sometimes you gain but you still have life to try again.

You know you can't always control

but one day you will find the way to end the show.

Who will ever understand your feelings when even you can't still catch them.

Don't try to find ones who think
that they can bear with you with attempts.

"Be kind, be free", they say
    "Be kind to yourself. It's always free", I say.

Like I'm trapped in my thoughts that drive me to think negative endlessly and forever caught

no matter how much I try to leave.

Writing it down never helps

even I stop myself from thoughts of storms but depression is still on my shelf

like a cancerous circle, I'll never be freed from.

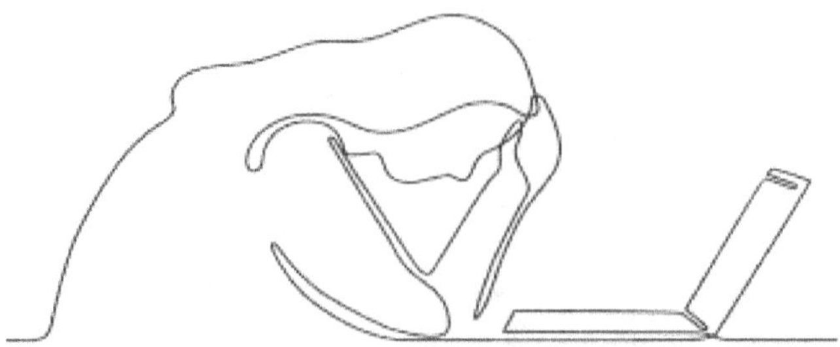

When you were young and fresh
people told you to run away from strangers but now who scares me the most
is this strange face
that chases me like dark shadow and clings to me forever.

They told me to throw away the past and to not worry about the future path Do as best as I can today

They say as if it was an easy way.
Yet, I know what to do to control it
but with depression makes it hard like tons of sh*t!

And why I'm still here, breathing it's because I still have many things
that I want to do and still hope, always I'll come back stronger one day
and smile and laugh when I beat
this monster like a king of war, and be pleased.

Living day by day is better than never breathing anymore.
I know I can be a shelter
for the lovers who never ask for even though I can't feel happiness
but the smallest things I do can also bring the pleasure to the people I love best
and that makes me feel something.

I'm a crumpled piece of paper
and thrown away because of this monster.
I didn't let it take me down
but can't say it's never full of clout.
Exercises can help, and you should
and I'm here with you in my workout suit.

Did I lose myself who can laugh?
    The one that shines and always smiles.
    The one that can be content with little stuff. Where are you, dear?
    Find her and I'll give a prize!

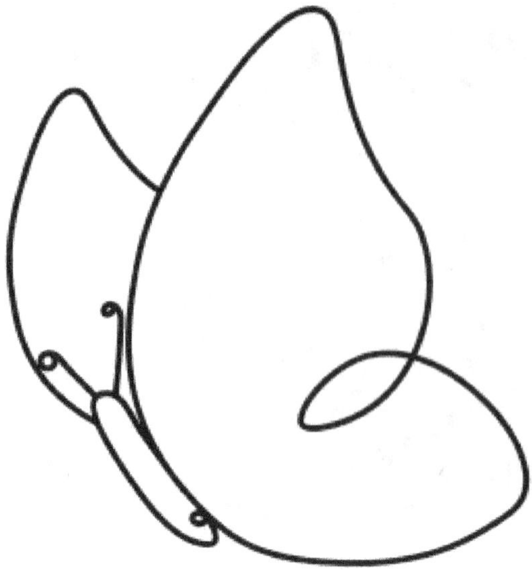

I know I've lost the old me even money can't take her back.
A million? It still can't do a wee.
A thousand million still can't get me back!

Who can know they are depressed?

...

Never

...

But at some point, you'll find yourself in a corner of being never happy with anything and anyone.

It's a strange feeling and you'll know once that depression is spreading over your body. It's out of clues when brain substances release

ABNORMALLY.

People will see and say that you've changed And yes! I hate it best as if it was a plague!

Many misunderstand and think depression comes from stress, the environment that shapes you,

or traumas you've been through.

But with no clues, some people have it in their chest and no one understands it best,

but I get you.

I can't even express my muffled cries just like a dead body that denies feeling.

I can't accept this deal in me and sympathize as I feel like I'm dying inside and being sealed.

"Be positive." That's what they say. and I yell, "Yes!' every time that they tell me what I should do to live

and I've been doing so to keep breathing alive just to let the day past

but when the night comes, I pray it'll go fast.

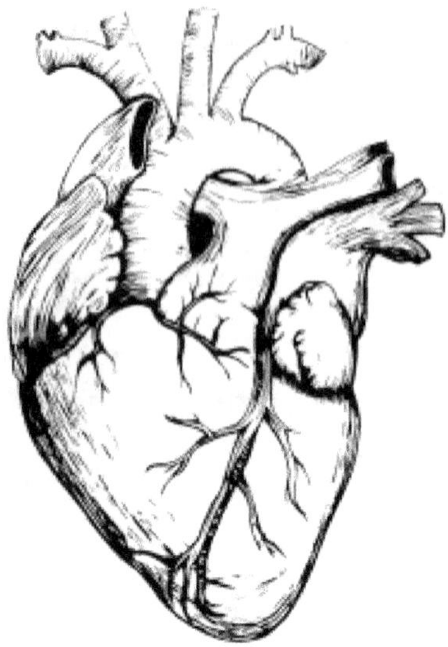

Just smile and don't be sad We're not glad to see you blue
and I grin and think I want to have fun so bad but serotonin is running mad, so I woo
I feel sorry I can't enjoy the fun
as depression is playing with me now.
I feel sorry I can't shine as the sun
and then I turn a run and leave the crowd.

I've lost count of my age
I felt empty like I was in a cage of loneliness, I'd never run away from, but I do hope my next birthday I'll feel better and depression ends
And shall never come back to me again.

We always appreciate good days and survive bad ones.

We always learn a ton from those good and bad times and we embrace them and appreciate those lessons.

At least you learn and gain something from these crimes.
Life always alters, and things always change day by day.
You can just play and enjoy every moment in your life.
We all might be in a book with fifty shades of grey,
so we just need to play our roles to the end of the line.

Sometimes you do what you don't want to. It is just to toil with your patience.

Nobody can force you to even do
things that you don't want to experience.

Death is a sure thing that waits for us

but I want to touch my happiness before I die just like when I was young, I smiled so much laughed and lived without any worries in mind. I'm trying harder for people around and me

I take medicine, work out, pray, and think

of positive things as they can make me feel free and hopeful that one day I'll get out of this thing.

Listening to your favorite songs, but it feels different and worse. This makes me feel so bad for long even favorite movies get me cursed. When you have this monster inside you might not feel the same way with what you ever loved and liked.

I feel nothing with what from old days.

You're doing better, better than what we've been through as if you were going to be
gone tomorrow.
So you don't have anything to regret for, do you? but please don't be stupid and do things
in sorrow.
Don't commit suicide or yourself killed.
I can see from the hill how much you suffer but believe me, believer, and be chill
that natural death feels so much cooler.

You can start over.

Don't think about and suffer with how long you have never felt happy, so grasp that it's just another bad day to your better day.

Learn to live with it, but not give a thing. It's easy to think and say, but you know you're strong, so you can still think

that you can try harder and leave the woe. You're vigorous to pick up this book and read and remember, this disease doesn't make you lonely

because not just you who's fighting this beast. At least you have me, and I'll be your company

:)

The night can never be longer. Every second runs slowly.
 Minutes seem like hours.
 It's because I can't sleep freely.

Talking is a good practice as it makes you feel relieved
when feelings are expressed in speech and I hope they listen and give
the sign that they understand me but with some people, it's no use even how much I try utterly.
They can't make me feel better and loose.

I was ever afraid to be fragile

but I'm a human who feels and cries who can get hurt and be in pain.

We can't turn against this natural chain.

So don't be afraid to feel weak sometimes just because mental illness is making you cry.

It's like I fell into a black hole dark, lonely, and hopeless

no matter how long time has gone no one knows I'm in this darkness.

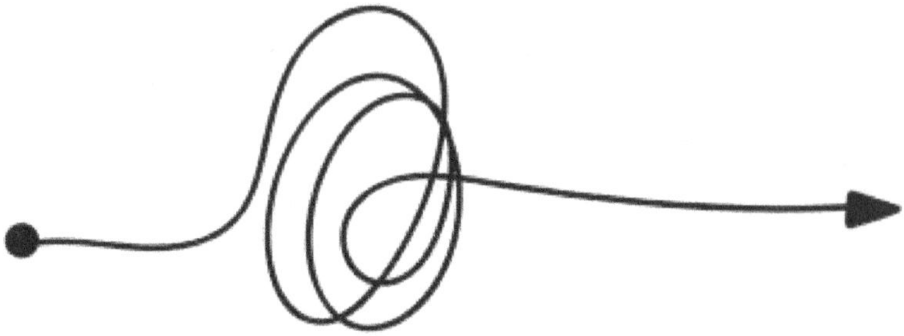

I know life is hard,
    But who knows it's even worse with this hurt disease, I start thinking long major depression is a curse.

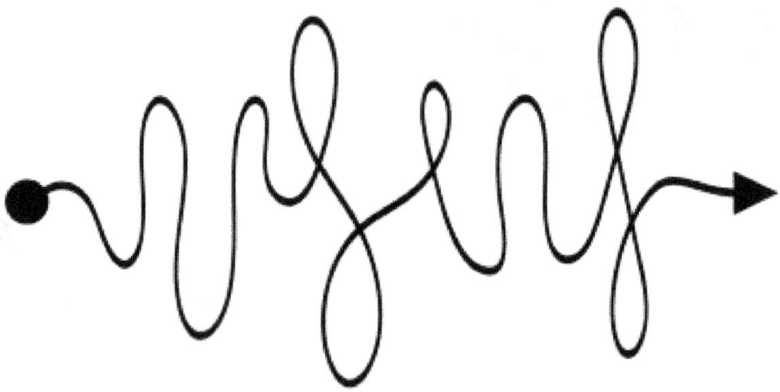

Been living with it for so long, I'm starting feeling it belongs to my soul for the whole life

but when getting through things, it seems like everything I've been through becomes soft without depression, as I feel like a corpse.

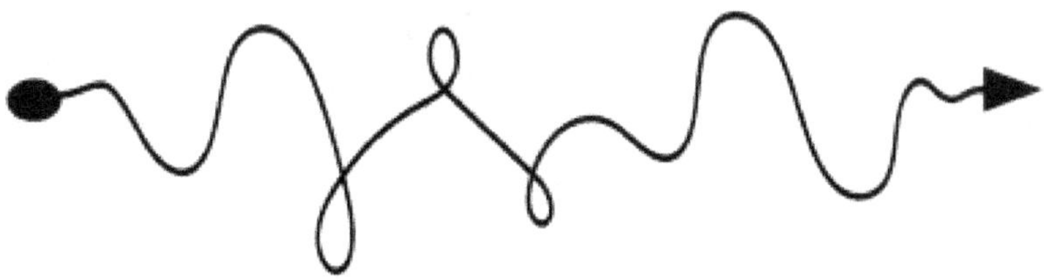

I was ever afraid of what they think of me but recently I'm afraid of myself more

as I can do the worst that from people will flee the thoughts inside my head are the best horror.

Love is always a good thing until you're heart-broken
and can't move on from thinking why you're here, broken.

Hesitation, confusion, and being indecisive are such a great time waster but it's what we need to do to keep best results you expect ever.

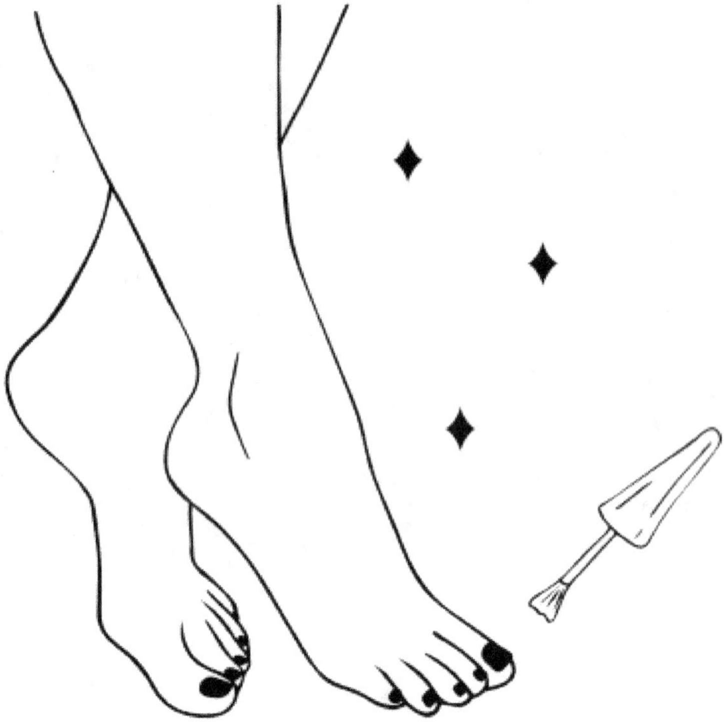

Your eyes that look at me when you know I'm not normal is the loudest silence of all.

Please don't look at me
like I'm a trash you'll throw free.

Gas and fire can't be together, dangerous just like me and my negative thoughts, I trust as finally, fire will burn all
just like me, hurting you all.

Be silent and breathe let the time goes by.
  This is not bad indeed
  just don't let myself go wild.

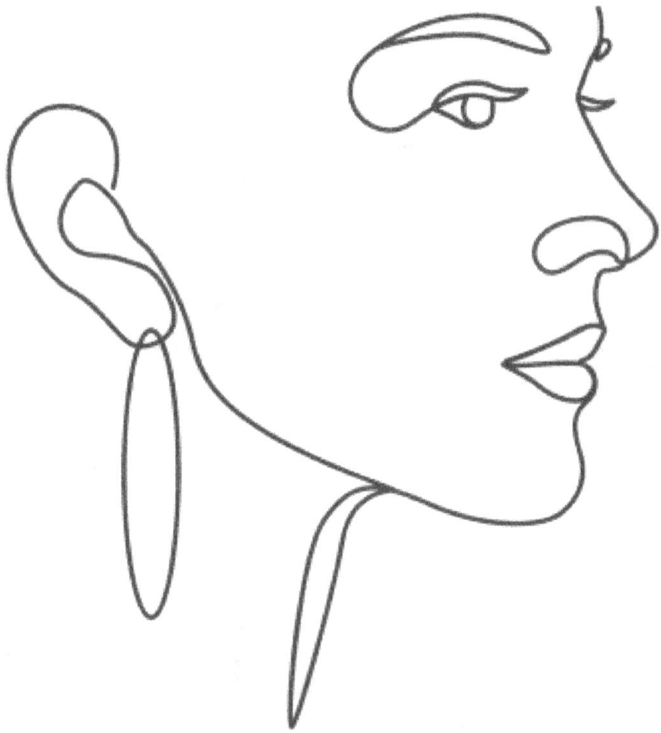

Stop pampering people and care for yourself love yourself and twirl
it's you who will forever be with you, I tell.

No one is perfect, and that's okay. You're not perfect, and that's very okay.

I think I'm looking forward, but not true, I'm just worried about things like a coward.

My future is so blurry.

Have you ever, ever looked at old pictures and seen that back then
how much you were happy and when things changed, and in some photos
you forced those smiles even when you felt zero.

The world moves on every day. Everybody moves on, also
I stand stupidly in this little hole
what a sh*t feeling to cope with, walk me away.

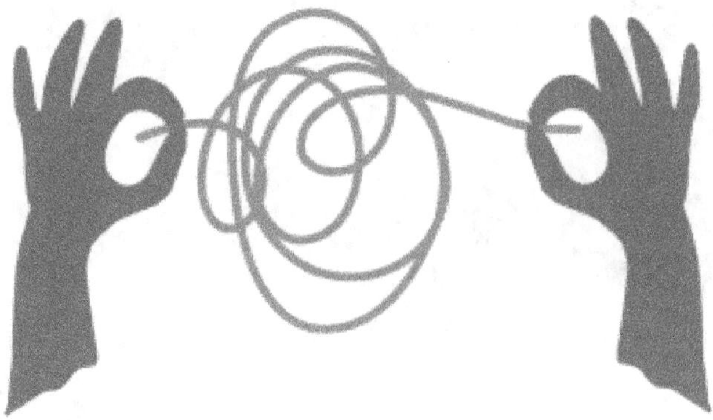

Depression is a villain with a criminal mind
hunting down people in pain but at the end, I'll survive.

"Hello, how are you?" is such a sick question that I never want to say anything back to the person.

You're finding every way to escape from this feeling
instead, get up and know one thing this is just the damn thought,
you say that you'll get through one day.

My moods are insecure, and so my life
    but what I feel is real
    even if it's killing me inside.

Comparing yourself to others can never cause greater
to you, the true enemy you need
to beat is yourself yesterday, indeed.

How sad we need to be to call it depression sometimes one doesn't need to be diagnosed with

but it's just losing the ability to feel happy at once
it's just you can't feel happy yourself, that's it.

My psychiatrist is so happy to see me and she says,
"We'll get through it together"
but deeply I don't want to see her a wee
yes, it's because I want now to get recovered.

Every hug used to get me better when I was sad but not with bad depression I'm bearing.

I'm sorry that I feel nothing,
but I'm still glad and a part of me, I feel grateful for those hugs,
I think.

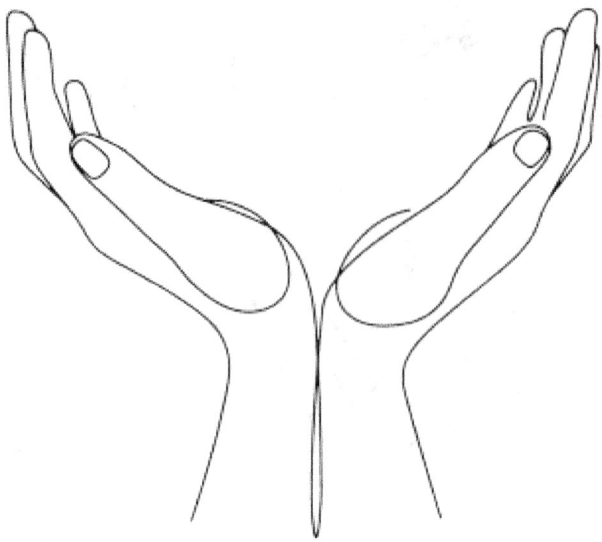

I can't read emotional news or even sentimental stories.

It's like hundred needles trying to kill and pricking my heart painfully every time I hear such bad things ...

In treatments, I'm aware I should avert from things that make me nervous and overthink

but I'm still human who has feelings and can be hurt and is it that wrong if I feel sympathetic

to people I've seen in such an unlucky Situation?

Then I know I'm pathetic

that I can't even express my feeling, poor me.

Time flies every day.

Each minute feels so long and never ends. Like no one can help, even I pray,

unleash me from imprisonment of this monster with strength.

Sometimes I just want to sleep, sleep, sleep, and sleep.
I wish I didn't wake up again to feel this cynical pain.

I go everywhere I pray every day
to recover from this shit, not fair!
I would go miles and miles away
to get out of this feeling, I shall say.

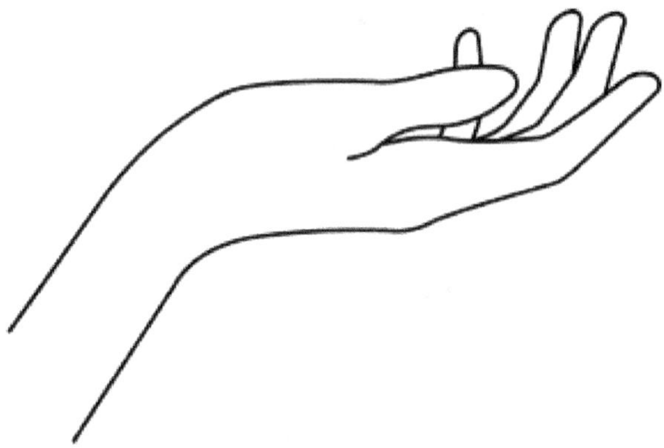

I'm messed up, who can't manage myself always confused and don't know what I desire I still have goals and want to follow as I tell but, all in all, I miss you by my side.

Many times that I've looked over the clock hands just as it is said, "Time heals", and you'll never know...

If that is eternally true, then tell me if I can buy all the 'ticks' in the world.

Blursday's become normal

as every day is so gloomy and all. Not a day can longer be important just like the heart that crushes and can

never get back to the same piece by piece Oh Lord, this is much painful, indeed.

I hope you will be with me all the time never leave me behind
always hold my hand and keep telling me "It will get better"
"We will move on from this together."

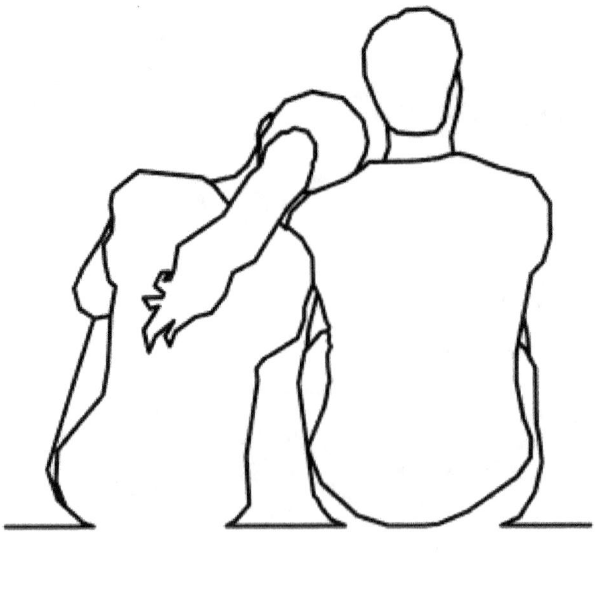

I want to hold your face and hug you tightly.
I promise I'll be the same me as soon
as possible, who can make you smile lovely
and don't worry about me. I love you to the moon.

Death has no fear
only we fear the fear itself death can't do me apart
because it is already with me all the time.

People who hurt themselves are fools who can do such stupid things
but sometimes we never know we also do those foolish things without even thinking.

You always cheer me up, darling every time that I call you
you always pick up and say, "**How are you doing?**"
and I know you don't want to get my calls so often
but I'm glad you still do that
as if you sat with me in the kitchen without any signs of annoyance.

Physical wounds can never compare to mental injuries.

I barely survive the pain that lasts forever as if it's cutting deep inside my body.

Not a day goes by without crying. My temper is swinging madly.

I want to scream out with all suffering but I'm just thinking as I breathe weakly.

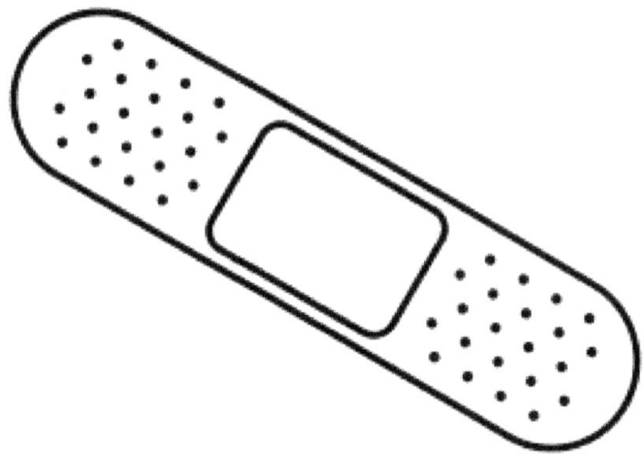

I feel thankful to all of you I met who gave the lessons, good and bad. I thank my friends, my love, my ex, my family, and strangers, I am glad you're always kind and merciful.

This might be my last word to all of you even though it's what I always say,

I'll keep telling you all this till my last day.

I shower, then take some sleeping pills and I let life pass another night.

That's the best way to get myself killed to live with depression all my life.

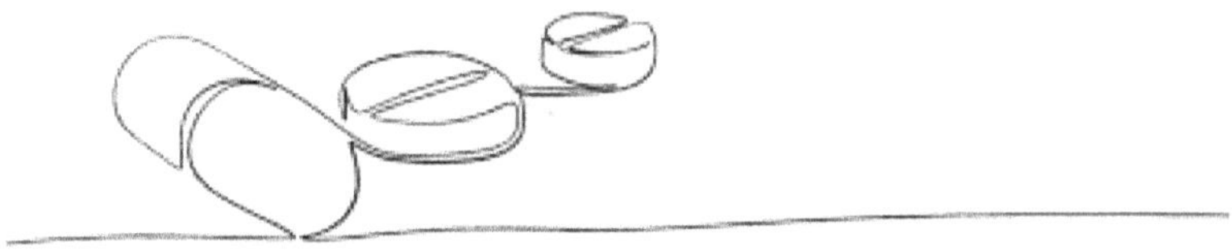

Your love keeps me alive my life keeps you smile
and both of us can actually try to smile and be alive together and I hope we'll last forever.

I don't have feelings for love I don't have feelings for sex
I don't have feelings for anything above Am I abnormal?
well, I feel weird. Let's check.

Please forgive me and my little mouth for always speaking the same thing that whether I'll pull out the sling
and kill this beast and get it out.

About recovery

:)

Thank you for rubbing my head before I'm going to bed.

I feel so warm and comfortable that now I still have you, people I love, and don't leave me alone

even you're in my dream of Jones.

I ever dreamed of the good life, being fulfilled in work and might have money and a good love

but the thing I care the most of all above is my health.

As if what happens to my life,

I can't help to build the life I desire

and that's not cool at all, so please, my body, stay healthy and wait together to see us happy again.

The taste of being an adult is bitter when people and strangers expect you to stand strong and don't ever show your weakness and defects. You're expected to handle things on your own and don't be messed even though sometimes just asking

for help is the thing you should do best.

Freedom happens when you just say, “F*ck this”, and then, “I’m done,” and walk away.

The one who hurts me the most is me so I'm giving myself determination

that one day I'll stop hurting myself completely. This is a vow from me to my better version.

Things always change, you know,
if you think this is the lowest point of your show things will get better soon, just believe
just like a graph of life that keeps going down and will eventually rise
don't surrender to the reluctance in this fight.

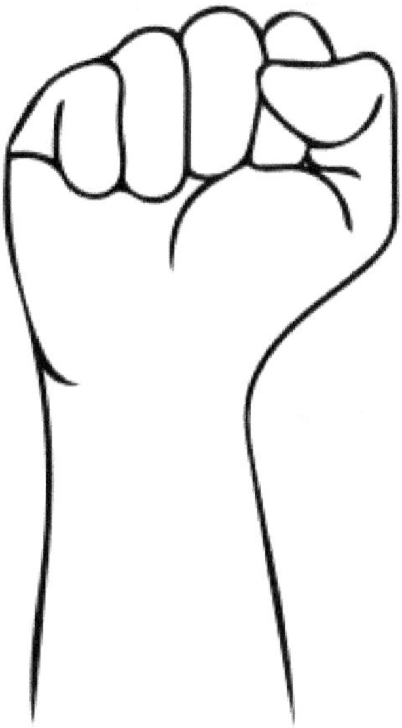

Stay with people who understand you but don't try to be toxic to them they're not doing anything sinful

It's just you who can't be tame.

I hope people with depression get better soon praying to the moon they'll feel normal

I excoriate the existence of this misfortune and call upon my wish it won't happen to all.

What doesn't kill you makes you stronger that's always been told to her by people

but she always struggles and prays for an offer. That it'd be better if it didn't come back in her cycle.

Please be gone for good.

Don't stop loving yourself
but stop keeping anyone else happy you're the first priority to tell that you care for yourself muchly.

Keep doing your job at your best even if it's not easy to do as said don't find yourself unoccupied as you may cry and go wild

go out and get some fresh air

do things that you like and don't care reluctance will find its way

and you'll get recovered in days.

Live your life best day by day and play with what you feel like
move your life forward along the way
and one day you'll feel okay from those stikes.

My heart is pounding so loud I can't now try to sleep

thinking if the panic attack is yet again around sometimes I'm afraid of death, then I weep.

What'd it be like after death But who knows that best?

Human is such a society of greed endlessly grinding to the top

life must go on, and if you're pleased with what you have, you can stop and be happy no matter how much the world is continually messed up.

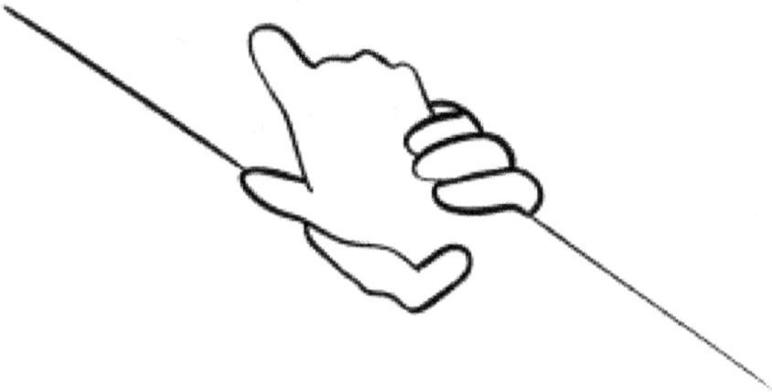

I believe that every illness comes from our behavior.

And most importantly, from our little thoughts when mindset changes the way of life, life alters be consistent and focused on what makes you joyous.

Even if it's just a small thing that can make you happy. Be proud that at least you can live freely.

I used to be afraid of living alone

I used to be afraid of being trouble to people with this mental illness.

But now it's well known and people seem more open,

but who truly knows your struggle?

Believe me, I don't really want to die but what I always wish is to get rid of this monstrous illness out of my mind and I finally hope I'll never have it.

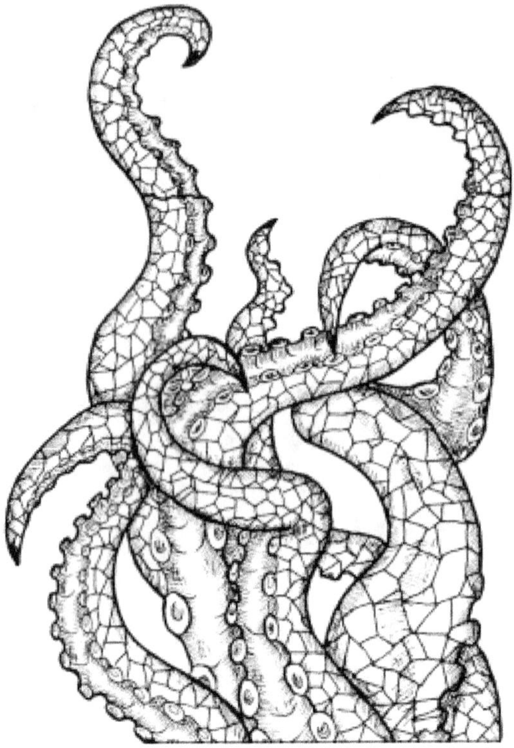

Competition leads to improvement in self, which is valuable, but on the other hand, we never have to strive to beat anyone else for a good, normal life, that we all can have as a basis. Hence, no one should be

So stressed with living their life, and also me.

Everyone can always start over

learning from the past, being focused on today planning for the best in the future.

You know when you were born, but not the day you die, so I'm doing everything at my best

to live my life every day with nothing to regret.

Love is an enigma, you know sometimes it comes into your life when you least expect so,

and you regret that timing isn't right.

Nothing is better than knowing yourself best so you can develop your strengths and winning points, and that starts from having courage.

When you can stand up against something, you have your half win, so please be faithful

and be brave. One day you'll achieve your goals.

Take a deep breath when you feel down then breathe out slowly, as it'll help decrease anxiety well and you'll know how to be focused on your breaths and yourself.

I feel better because of medicine and changing my obsession
I work out a lot, eat clean,
and avoid sweets as they cause inflammation.

Everything happens for a reason
I've learned a lot from having depression
I've never ever wanted to deal with this demon and I want you to know that you're so strong and not abandoned as I'm also here with you
to be your company and feel what you've been through.

www.ingramcontent.com/pod-product-compliance
Lightning Source LLC
LaVergne TN
LVHW022229200926
848481LV00006B/2194